LANDSCAPE DETECTIVE

Alison Hawes

Published 2009 by
A & C Black Publishers Ltd.
36 Soho Square, London, W1D 3QY
www.acblack.com

ISBN HB 978-1-4081-0859-8
    PB 978-1-4081-1288-5

Series consultant: Gill Matthews

Text copyright © 2009 Alison Hawes

Produced for A & C Black by Calcium.
Printed and bound in China by C&C Offset Printing Co.

Acknowledgements
The publishers would like to thank the following for their kind permission to reproduce their photographs:
Cover: Shutterstock. **Pages:** Corbis: Gideon Mendel 12; Istockphoto: Bart Coenders 5, Jami Garrison 7tc, Robert Adrian Hillman 6r, Linda Steward 6c; Science Photo Library: Cordelia Molloy 16t; Shutterstock: Pontus Edenberg 7tl, Joerg Humpe 10t, juliengrondin 20, kavram 10br, Jacques Kloppers 15cl, Olga Lyubkina 14, MaxFX 13br, Tan Wei Ming 4, Luciano Mortula 15cr, Edyta Pawlowska 7bg, Mark William Richardson 15b, Karen Roach 17c, Fred Sweet 21, Stephen VanHorn 6l, Viktoriya 17b, Feng Yu 8c, Sergiy Zavgorodny 8t. **Illustrations:** Geoff Ward 9, Emma DeBanks 14t, 18–19.

The author would like to thank Rachel Wall, Head of Geography, Angmering School, West Sussex for her invaluable help and advice whilst researching this title.

Contents

Landscape Detectives

Anyone can be a landscape detective.
All you need is:

1. An interest in the world around you.

2. The right tools for the job.

Landscape detectives are interested in places and people. They are interested in weather, **habitats**, and the environment.

Sometimes, landscape detectives **investigate** places and people close to where they live.

Sometimes, they investigate people and places further away.

These detectives are finding out what is happening to the **rainforest**.

To investigate the world around them, landscape detectives need to:

⇨ ask questions

⇨ gather evidence

⇨ look for clues

⇨ investigate why things happen

⇨ take measurements

A LANDSCAPE DETECTIVE'S TOOLKIT

- maps
- photographs
- digital camera
- video camera
- notebook
- clipboard
- compass
- laptop
- click wheel
- rain gauge
- thermometer
- anemometer
- books
- dvds and the internet

Is your landscape changing?

Keep a photographic record of all new buildings, or old ones being pulled down. You can then look back at them to see how the landscape has changed.

Landscape detectives have many tools to help them investigate. Read on to find out how and when to use these tools.

Maps

Different maps give different kinds of information. Always read the title on a map, so that you choose the right map for the type of information you want.

DETECTIVE DOS AND DON'TS

DO Fold a map carefully when you have finished with it.

KNOW YOUR MAPS

Road maps
Use these when making or tracking long journeys.

Old maps
Use these to see how a place used to look.

Street maps
Use these when making or tracking short journeys.

Scale

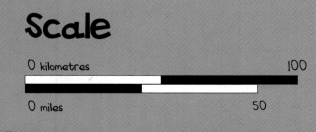

0 kilometres   100

0 miles   50

Maps are drawn to different scales. The **scale** is shown on the scale bar.

Always choose a map with the right scale for the type of information you want.

Atlases

Use these when looking at different countries in detail.

Large-scale maps

Use these when looking at the landscape in detail.

Globes →

Use these to locate countries and seas around the world.

REMEMBER!

A *small*-scale map shows a *large* area of land.

Using Maps

To help you use a map, you need to know about the points of a compass, so you can follow directions.

You also need to know about grids, keys, and symbols so you can find places on a map more easily.

Compasses

A compass is a tool that helps you find and follow directions.

An eight point compass →

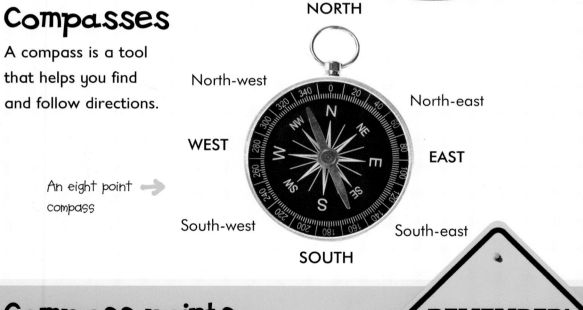

NORTH

North-west

North-east

WEST

EAST

South-west

South-east

SOUTH

Compass points

The main points on a four point compass are North, South, East, and West.

REMEMBER!
Most maps are drawn with North at the top.

Grids

Most maps have a grid
of squares drawn on them.
On some maps each square
is given a number or a letter.
On some maps each line of
the grid is given two numbers.

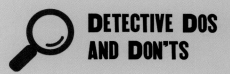

DETECTIVE DOS AND DON'TS

DO Practise your map-reading skills
with real maps. When you
next go out for the day, see
if you can track your bus, car,
or train journey on a map.

FIND THE STREET

My house is on Rogate Road
in square B5.

To find my street:
Move your finger east,
along the bottom of the
map. Stop at square B.
Now move your finger
north to square 5.

9

Map Keys and Symbols

The key is the most important part of a map. It is the tool that tells you what all the symbols and colours on a map mean.

Always look at the key on a map. Maps hold lots of information but the key unlocks that information.

This map symbol shows you where a railway station is.

This map symbol shows you where marshland is.

TRY IT OUT!

Try the online map games at:

mapzone.ordnancesurvey.co.uk

Symbols

The symbols on a map can show you what a landscape looks like and what is on that land. Some symbols are simple pictures or shapes. Maps must show a lot of information, but there is not enough room on them for lots of labels. So symbols are used instead.

KNOW YOUR SYMBOLS

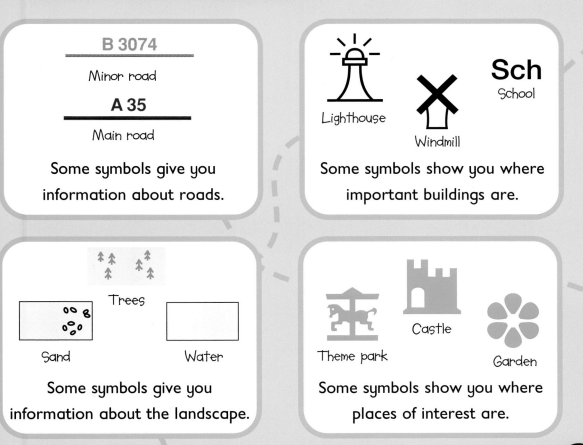

B 3074

Minor road

A 35

Main road

Some symbols give you information about roads.

Lighthouse
Windmill
Sch
School

Some symbols show you where important buildings are.

Trees
Sand
Water

Some symbols give you information about the landscape.

Theme park
Castle
Garden

Some symbols show you where places of interest are.

Photographs

Photographs are a good tool. They can help you learn more about the places and people around you. Landscape detectives use photographs taken from the ground and from the air.

Looking for clues

Photos taken at different times of year might show you how places and people are affected by things like:

⇨ weather

⇨ pollution

⇨ tourism

This **aerial photograph** shows land affected by flooding.

Asking questions

A photograph can hold a lot of information. To find out that information, landscape detectives ask questions about the photographs they use.

⇨ Where were these photographs taken?

⇨ When were they taken?

⇨ What changes can you see in the photos?

⇨ Why have things changed?

⇨ Who has been affected by these changes?

⇨ How have they been affected?

TRY IT OUT!

Look for maps and photos of where you live online at Geograph or Google Maps or Windows Live local. **www.geograph.org.uk**

Ice in the Arctic

Photographs taken from space over time show that ice is melting in the Arctic. ⇨

REMEMBER!

Look for old photographs of where you live at your local museum.

13

Gathering Evidence

Landscape detectives have different ways of gathering **evidence**.

A field sketch

Field sketch

A field sketch is a drawing of the place you are investigating. Always label your sketch and give it a title.

You will need a:

⇨ **clipboard**
⇨ **paper**
⇨ **pencil**
⇨ **rubber**
⇨ **a good pair of eyes!**

This landscape detective is recording what he finds with his camera.

Survey

When doing a **survey**, make a table of the questions you are going to ask,

OR

of the things you are going to be finding out.

DETECTIVE DOS AND DON'TS

Before you use a digital camera:
DO Check there is room on the memory card.
DO Check the battery is charged.

Cameras

Using a camera is an easy way of collecting evidence. Digital cameras are simple to use. They keep your pictures on a memory card and don't use film.

You could take pictures of the different types of houses that you see where you live, or where you go on holiday.

15

Tools for Measuring

Landscape detectives also use tools for measuring things such as distance and the weather. Taking measurements is another way landscape detectives gather evidence.

Distance

Short lengths and depths can be measured in centimetres or millimetres with a ruler. Longer distances can be measured with a **click wheel**. The number of clicks counted show how far you have travelled.

Rainfall

The tool for measuring rainfall is a **rain gauge**. It is a special plastic pot with a spike on the end. The spike is pushed into the ground to stop the gauge blowing away. Rain falls into the gauge and the amount is measured in millimetres.

↑ Every time you hear a click the click wheel has travelled 1 m.

REMEMBER!

Don't put the rain gauge near buildings or trees that might shelter it from the rain.

Temperature

The temperature of the air is measured with a **thermometer**.

TRY IT OUT!

You can make you own tools for measuring weather. See how to at:

www.bbc.co.uk/weather/ weatherwise

Wind

You measure wind speed with an **anemometer**.

An anemometer measures wind speed in kmh.

Displaying Information

Landscape detectives try to display the information they have collected, so it is easy for everyone to understand. Some information is best displayed as a map or a plan. Other information is easier to understand if it is displayed as a diagram or graph.

Maps and plans

A map or plan is a good way of displaying information about a journey or a place.

MY School

The railway

← This is a map of my journey to school.

Steep hill going down

The Playing fields

The church

My House

The Village Hall

Graphs

A graph can be a good way to display the results of a survey. A graph makes it easier to understand the results. You can draw a graph on paper. Or you can draw a graph with the help of a computer program.

Diagrams

A diagram is a good way of displaying how something happens or how something works.

↓ This diagram shows what happens when we recycle paper.

These graphs show how a group of children travel to school. The *same* information is shown in three *different* ways.

Walking
Driving
Cycling

Pictograph

Bar graph

Pie chart

Searching for Information

Two of the best places a landscape detective can use to search for information are the library and the internet.

Using the library

To find an information book in the library, look in the non-fiction section. All the books on these shelves are sorted by topic. This is so you can find what you are looking for more easily. Each non-fiction book also has a number on its spine. All the books on the same topic have the same number on the spine. A librarian can tell you which number to look for to find the information you want.

In the library you can find out about volcanoes by looking for books starting with the number 551.21.

Using the internet

To find information on the internet, type a question or some keywords into the search box. This will bring up a list of websites. Click on the websites to find the information you want.

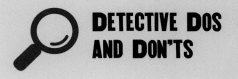

⬆ The internet gives you instant access to information from around the world.

Glossary

aerial photograph a photograph taken from the air

anemometer a tool for measuring the speed of the wind

click wheel a tool for measuring long distances

evidence information

habitat where something lives

investigate to search and find out

rainforest a forest in a hot country that receives a lot of rain

rain gauge a tool for measuring how much rain has fallen

scale the scale of a map, shows how much the real size of
a place has been shrunk to fit on a map.

survey an investigation

thermometer a tool for measuring temperature

Further Information

Websites

For information about maps, photographs, and great games go to:
http://mapzone.ordnancesurvey.co.uk/mapzone

For information about landscapes and practising map skills go to:
www.bbc.co.uk/scotland/education/sysm/landscapes

Lots of information about the Earth, maps, and weather can be found at:
www.kidsgeo.com/geography-for-kids/index.php

Find out all about the weather and its effect on people at:
www.bbc.co.uk/schools/whatisweather

Books

Maps and Mapping by Deborah Chancellor. Kingfisher (2004).

Just the Facts: World Atlas by Dee Phillips. Ticktock (2006).

Follow the Map: Car Journey by Deborah Chancellor. Franklin Watts (2005).

Index